THINK DIFFERENT

PERSEVERANCE WITH HOPE IS
POWER

Kawtar Louahbi

Mariem Mouhsine

CONTENTS

PERSEVERANCE WITH HOPE IS...i

POWER i

LET'S START AGAIN FROM THE END ix

LET'S TURN OBSTACLES INTO CHALLENGES....................................... xi

THE GAME WON'T CHANGE UNLESS YOU CHANGE THE CARDS...................... 1

THE ENEMIES OF SUCCESS..3

THE ACCUSER 4

THE SELF-DOUBTER 7

THE MOANER..9

THE NARCISSIST 10

THE PETER PAN 11

THE STONY FACED... 13

LET'S START WITH OURSELVES 14

TAKING RESPONSIBILITY 16

FOR OUR ACTIONS 16

THE MORNING ROUTINE 18

CALLING PEOPLE BY THEIR NAME 20

SMILE, SMILE, SMILE 21

EMBRACING DIVERSITY... 22

CHANGE IS THE ONLY POSSIBLE WAY 24

THINK DIFFERENT

LET'S START AGAIN FROM THE END

Hell is that state where one has ceased to hope.
A. J. Cronin

Who hasn't had difficult experiences in life? Each one of us has known frustrating moments when the desire to give up seemed irreversible, and when the smile gradually faded.

What makes us different from anyone else is the way we face the ups and downs of the great roller coaster that is life. Sometimes, however, we happen to fall, and not find the strength to get back on our feet. My story is one such case.

Perhaps no one is allotted a simple path, but I can certainly claim that I wasn't granted any shortcuts. Today, when I think back of the past, I can clearly see how many disappointments and how many blows life has dealt me.

I still can't pinpoint for sure when it happened; however, at some point I realized that weren't it for the blows I had suffered, not only would I not have had the strength to get back up on my feet, but I wouldn't have found the courage to change – an outcome that now looks priceless. And it is precisely thanks to this change, that I can now look back on my life not with the anger of someone trapped in frustration, but rather with a touch of sweetness that almost resembles gratitude.

No matter how many times I felt tired or discouraged, it's thanks to those moments that I understood and internalized what my life path is. I know, we can't help but wonder what may be the secret to always find the strength to carry on, and never give up. In fact, is there such a secret at all?

Well, as far as I'm concerned, I think there is. My whole experience does nothing but repeat a very specific word to me; it keeps reminding me that what has always provided me with the strength to go on, is hope.

Hope is like a rainbow that comes after a storm to remind us that beauty exists. It is what separates the unfortunate fallen on the battlefield – who could not find in themselves the strength to carry on and overcome their fears – from those who threw their hearts over the fence, and can finally look back from beyond the abyss.

We all hope for a brighter future. We all hope to achieve at least some of the goals we have set for ourselves. However, it may happen that our fear of the future – in other words, fear of the unknown – crushes our hope and expectations. When this happens, it's fear itself that becomes our number one enemy, our biggest obstacle. It puts a spoke in our wheel, pollutes our dreams and turns off the light on our path, making us increasingly pessimistic about the future that lies ahead.

I hope that I was able to pour sincere and straightforward advice into these pages, for the benefit of anyone who feels lost. Just as lost as I used to feel. I hope that my words can be of real help for those who fight against adversity but want – stubbornly want – to continue on their path, despite any difficulties.

I dedicate my little book to all who always strive to see the glass half full; to those who find the strength and courage to smile at yet another door slammed in their face; to the people who have lost their way, and doubt whether they can ever find it again; and those who always find themselves back at the starting point, despite all their sacrifices.

I hope that my thoughts can stir just a little something, somewhere deep down inside of them. Because, after all, even the largest of fires starts from a tiny spark.

LET'S TURN OBSTACLES INTO CHALLENGES

We are disturbed not by things,
but by the view which we take of them.
Epictetus

Hope is the beginning of the ascent, the so-called "success" axiom. Let's take children, for instance. They are the ones who hold the secret to how we can believe in our dreams in an unwavering way. The age of childhood still keeps them safe from the constraints that society is eager to impose.

They can spread so much positive energy, can't they? They are impatient; they want to grow quickly to realize their projects; they have an indomitable will to learn, and are not deterred by obstacles.

Their need to explore is inherent, and soon they start crawling just to be able to discover new spaces around them. Their instinct won't let them be satisfied. Next, they want to learn to walk, and then to run. But before they do it, they will stagger, fall, get up, and fall again. For a while they will seemingly give up and resume crawling, but in fact they will only be digesting all their newly gathered information, and licking their wounds. And now they are ready to try all over again: they cling to the sofa or to a chair, and face the unknown one more time. That's what we've all done, even though we don't remember it.

Over time, inevitably our difficulties increase. But why shouldn't we continue to have that same approach, and the same determination we had as children?

As we grow up, we develop new skills, acquire complex notions, face new experiences and certainly make mistakes. Let's face it: it is the very process of growth that reminds us of our ability to understand the nature of the obstacle before us. We all have what it takes to analyze problems in the most suitable way, as well as to address and overcome them with the least possible damage. In this process, hope is for us what gasoline is for a car. It's what makes us move.

Now, let's try to focus on our problems: what might happen if we no longer considered them to be unsolvable dilemmas or unbearable burdens, but rather opportunities? Shifting our point of view, and looking at problems as challenges, changes everything. Our brain spontaneously gears up to look for new solutions, new ideas. More than just that: we shake off all those negative ruminations which feed our apprehension and our fears, all those "ifs" and "buts" that we ourselves put into play.

This is exactly the role of hope. Hope is the state of mind that lends us the courage to take off again, no matter how serious the circumstances may be. Hope is that split second that allows us to change the way we approach any obstacles, and to turn problems into challenges!

We live in the hope that our tomorrow will be better, and with the certainty that nothing is impossible so long as we have the determination and strength to not give up. How many things that we take for granted today, would have seemed like a miracle just yesterday? How would our grandparents react if they could see us speaking on the cell phone? Indeed, anything is possible. Just believe it! Just trust it.

THE GAME WON'T CHANGE UNLESS YOU CHANGE THE CARDS

*You can't expect to see change
if you never do anything differently.*
Albert Einstein

There is a bitter truth we cannot hide from: in order to change our lifestyle, wishful thinking is not enough. Nothing sorts itself out by magic.

Change is a profound process which must be analyzed, understood, assimilated, and then gradually implemented. With perseverance, above all.

I remember a story that I was told by my mentor. It really hit home with me. Adam was a difficult-tempered 18-year-old. He struggled to engage with other people. So much so that his parents – frustrated for not being able to help him – soon started to despair.

One day Adam's father, tired of his son's obstructive attitude, asked a wise friend for advice. As suggested by his friend, the father gave Adam a handful of nails and told him to drive one of the nails into the garden fence every time he mistreated someone.

Adam hammered so many of those nails in, that his arm soon began to ache! For weeks, he continued to hammer nail after nail, until – to the amazement of the whole family – the number of nails he hammered slowly began to decrease. Finally, the day came when Adam didn't hammer even a single nail into the fence.

Delighted with himself, the boy showed his great achievement to his father. Incredulous but proud, the father then moved on to the second part of the plan. Whenever Adam made a kind gesture to someone, he could remove one nail.

Adam was learning that a smile, a kind word, or an outstretched hand to help others, not only allowed him to remove those hideous nails from the fence, but made him a better person.

Only when he began to gradually change himself, did Adam see how others reacted positively to his change, and in turn changed their attitude towards him.

What Adam did, spurred on by his father, was transform a problem into a challenge, and then tackle it with an appropriate strategy, consistently and in small steps. Results weren't long in coming!

There's a moral to every story, and I hope this one can be at least as inspiring to you as it was to me.

To make change happen, we can only start with ourselves! It's our job to do it. At first, it may seem like we have a mountain ahead of us; but then, one step calls for another, and self-awareness increases.

Let's think of charismatic people, of all those who have found the way to establish themselves. Do we really believe it can be just a matter of luck? Not at all. It is rather the result of personal growth efforts.

As I said before, besides the fine words, in these pages I would like to propose some practical suggestions, some measures that can be implemented in everyday life. I will start doing this by focusing on some negative attitudes to improve.

THE ENEMIES OF SUCCESS

There are attitudes that more than others damage us by forcing us to deviate from the path of success. Unfortunately, they are also quite common. They are attitudes that feed on negativity, and that over time cause counter-productive feelings. One such case, for example, is the anger that often lurks inside of us, and that seemingly without reason erupts in inappropriate situations. These attitudes constitute invisible but very real chains that hinder our natural path.

At first glance, they may seem like simple ordinary habits, not unlike many others; yet in the long run their effect is to trap us – in spite of ourselves – into authentic prisons. I am convinced that by putting the spotlight on them, we may finally see them for what they really are: insidious behavioral traps. This can help us gain a clear awareness of purpose, and then adopt the right strategies to reduce their perceived effect upon us. Let's see what these attitudes are, and analyze them.

- The accuser

- The insecure

- The moaner

- The narcissist

- The Peter Pan

- The stony faced

THE ACCUSER

The journey of a thousand miles begins with one step.
Lao Tzu

The accuser is he who constantly blames others for his mistakes. Whenever we place the blame on others, it is as if we are telling our subconscious that we don't need it; that we are able to find a solution even without its contribution.

Regrettably, I was a real champion at blaming others. I blamed my parents for scolding me, and my professors for my poor grades. Everyone resented me! Their preferences always laid with others. I had given up hope: luck never knocked on my door. Bad luck and I were twins separated at birth: this was my personal motto. I blamed my friends for not having fun when I went out with them. I blamed my boss if – after just a few months working for him – he still hadn't recognized my outstanding professional skills. How could he not notice me? What a fool!

Unwittingly, I lived with this attitude for years. Then one day, looking in the mirror, I felt like I was staring into the cosmic void. I began to wonder where this life filled with pent-up frustration would take me. I realized that I had to take matters into my own hands.

To obtain different results and be successful, it is not enough to have a well laid out plan, nor to invest a hefty capital. Of course, there are always exceptions, just like winning the lottery.

In reality, true change begins with ourselves, exactly at the precise moment when we alter how we interpret the information coming from the outside. This is conscious change! And it's the kind of change whose backlash won't be devastating in the event of a temporary failure, since we'll have understood the rules of the game.

By transforming the way we see things, our vital drive changes too. We begin to see the world through different eyes. Even our breath and heart rate change. Things start to make more sense. We will look at the blows of our past in a new light. We'll have become aware that those mistakes were necessary to shape the person we are today. And it's precisely at that point, that the new results will materialize.

Another story that I find very meaningful is about a keen young boy, who had been dreaming from an early age of changing the world. He tried with all his might, but after many attempts he decided to downsize and aim to change his country instead. He threw himself headlong into this new adventure, but soon found himself stranded again, as changing an entire country seemed an almost impossible undertaking. He then focused his attention on his own neighborhood, but still without success. On the verge of giving up, he decided to further restrict his field of action to just his own family. Would it work this time? No! On the contrary, he found that changing even a dozen people was far too complicated. In the meantime, he had grown old, and he realized that the secret of change lies in starting with oneself.

Had he tried as a young boy to kick off change starting with himself, the people around him would have acknowledged the transformation, and spontaneously followed in his wake. This is how it works: over time, small changes engage more and more people. By doing so, from his neighborhood the young boy might have reached the rest of the world!

In order to make our dreams come true, it is necessary to start from ourselves.

Let's now analyze this mechanism: how does our brain interpret the concept of blaming others?

Well, when we are faced with a problem, our brain does its best to find a solution using the skills it has acquired during our lifetime. The natural course, in fact, is to learn as we grow, by identifying and implementing new solutions all the time. We learn to take responsibility, and we also grow on an interpersonal level. Life is a path, and it is only normal that we should encounter obstacles along the way.

By placing the blame on others, all we do is ignore this natural process by inhibiting and disarming our own brain, until it's no longer able to do its job. Jeez, it's someone else's fault anyway!

The unfortunate consequence of such a disruption of our natural functioning mechanism is that we stop learning from our mistakes, and thus improving.

It's the small steps that make the difference.

THE SELF-DOUBTER

From an early age, we have been victims of a blunder.

Don't we all remember when our mothers never passed on the opportunity to compare their respective children? Sooner or later, we all have tasted the bitterness of feeling inferior to others. Not only is the neighbor's grass always greener, but the neighbor's child is also smarter and more charismatic than our own.

Making comparisons, however, isn't always an attitude of which we are just helpless victims. Sometimes we are the ones who bear the guilt. Let's face it: how many times have we compared the skills of a classmate or work colleague to ours?

However, comparing ourselves to others is a tricky trap. The mechanism of comparison itself is misleading. Why? Because whenever we compare one of our deficiencies, we rub salt into the wound of this specific shortcoming. Hopelessly comparing ourselves with someone who excels in a certain field or in a certain quality, does nothing but damage our self-esteem, and makes us feel like losers.

However, there is a comparison that is not at all treacherous. It's the comparison with ourselves. Comparing our present self with our past self is a healthy exercise to face our limits, and to appreciate the progress we have made.

Indeed, one of the secrets of self-improvement is to impartially observe our progress over time. It's like running a marathon: the winner will be an athlete who focuses on the course and on how his body responds to the different stages of the race, in order to adjust his breathing, his speed, and so on. On the other hand, any athlete who won't stop obsessing over his competitors – the ones behind him, and the ones before him – will never come first!

Looking at ourselves first is an attitude that we should cultivate from an early age. In this respect, it is imperative that parents should not make the fatal error of comparing their children to other people's children. The risk of causing emotional waste in the child is very high. The apprehension caused by constant comparison will only fuel insecurities and uncertainties.

If we valued diversity, we would understand that it is completely normal not to excel in every field. We are all different, each with our own unique set of skills and inclinations. Let's leave comparisons outside the front door.

THE MOANER

Be kind, for everyone you meet is fighting a hard battle.
Plato

Let me start by saying that, as a woman, I used to love complaining. I could have earned a master's degree in this field.

Unfortunately, this is just yet another counter-productive attitude. Often our complaints turn into criticism of others. It's not pleasant to be criticized by others, is it? But let's ask ourselves why criticism makes us suffer. Usually, criticism casts a spotlight on some angle of our personality that we are not particularly proud of. As a consequence, we feel uncomfortable and activate our natural defenses – including, for example, retaliation.

If others see us as a source of constant criticism, they will defend themselves. Why on earth should we blame them for this?

There is a technique that allows us to mitigate this negative attitude. Let's call it the four-to-one technique. What is it all about? Basically, we should pay four compliments for every one criticism that we utter.

I would also like to make a final consideration on the so-called "constructive criticism". Well, I don't think there's any such thing. Criticism triggers negative emotions and causes discomfort and distress in the recipient – always, even when it is uttered with the best of intentions. Why not just give advice instead? Making people uncomfortable is never the solution.

THE NARCISSIST

I could more easily forgive his vanity had he not wounded mine. Jane
Austen

At the opposite end of the spectrum from the moaners, we can find the self-proclaimed rising stars of the solar system. Indeed, this is how they feel!

Being confident is a very good thing; but, as with all things, being excessively so is harmful.

The ironic side of the matter is that when we are dealing with an egocentric individual – that is, someone who always wants to be the center of attention, and only ever talks about him- or herself – we indulge them for a while; but then comes the moment when we want to escape, because deep down each one of us feels just as important. It almost annoys us that the talk isn't about us too!

A leading German telecommunications company conducted a study to identify the most used word in the world during phone conversations. Can you guess the answer? Unsurprisingly, it turned out to be the word "I". It featured 3,995 times across 5,000 calls. Astonishing, isn't it?

An episode from my own experience concerns a friend I met a few days ago, whom I had not seen for some time. For about twenty minutes, she did nothing but talk about herself; after which, upon realizing how much time had passed, she apologized for having talked incessantly. She seemed mortified. But no sooner had she finished her apology, that she was at it all over again, talking about herself. Obviously, leopards do not change their spots!

THE PETER PAN

When I think of the passing of time, I cannot help but remember Luciano De Crescenzo in Thus Spoke Bellavista, when he explained to his two amusing disciples that for Socrates "the past is no more and the future is not yet."

Past and future do not exist; the only time we can truly live in, is the present.

Yet many of us are constantly returning to their past, anchored to memories and to how things were. Despite all their efforts, however, there is no way they will be able to change past events. So, why devote it so much energy?

Life is a gift – the best gift we could ever have hoped for! Every day we have the power to change the present, and the future with it. It's not important if this requires small or big deeds, it's the intent that matters.

We have only one life, and the games will end with it. Choosing inaction and living a dull life is an insult to the very reason why we are here.

The past has the valuable function of providing us with memory, knowledge and skills, so that we can use them when the time comes. It is a sort of archive of the mind. What it can, and must, do for us is to help improve our future!

Life is a constant cycle of improvement, a totally fascinating mechanism.   Let's relive the past with all its experiences, but let's do it without forgetting our mistakes - or rather, with the intention to reconnect with their teachings, and to make a concrete use of them today. Our tomorrow will thank us for doing so.

THE STONY FACED

*It is requisite for the relaxation of the mind
that we make use, from time to time,
of playful deeds and jokes St.*
Thomas Aquinas

I knew a university professor whose voice and countenance were so dull, that on more than one occasion I felt an irresistible urge to get up, grab him by the shoulders and shake hard, just to see if he was really still alive.

Smiling is free. And it doesn't hurt to take life with a little lightness. Things and people around us will spontaneously conform to this spirit, just like the musical instruments get in tune with the orchestra.

One study has shown that newborns smiles more than four hundred times a day. As grown-ups, their smiles will plummet to less than twenty a day. Why?

Smiling requires us to activate fourteen facial muscles; on the contrary, we need as many as eighty to frown. Smiling is a way of life, and it requires some good will on our part. Smiling helps prevent stress. Above all, it allows us to always see the glass half full. That's not to be discounted!

LET'S START WITH OURSELVES

The only person you are destined to become
is the person you decide to be.'
Ralph Waldo Emerson

We all have experienced waking up in the morning in an excellent mood, full of energy, and keen to put it to good use; but then, unexpectedly, we crash into the exact opposite sensation, as if a dark veil had been cast over our best intentions. What is the matter?

For no apparent reason, sadness and gloom suddenly strike. Everything looks gray and meaningless. It's a horrible feeling, and unfortunately I know it well.

Although its exact origin can change from person to person, the general rule is that this is an alarm signal sent from our body to warn us that something is not right. Its purpose is to call our attention to the problem, because it's clear that we are too distracted or busy to deal with it.

Of course, this is a complex topic that would deserve a separate analysis, but here we can at least focus on some tricks to overcome the impasse. In the spirit of this e-book, I'm going to provide some practical advice that can make a real difference in the most sensitive situations, such as in the middle of a meeting or an exam.

People who know me, often ask how I can always be happy; how I can possibly be free of negative emotions.

No matter what difficulties I'm going through, from the moment that I go out in the morning, I forget the word "problem". I do it methodically. I focus exclusively on the person I'm interacting with, and never forget to start with a friendly "good morning!".

A lighthearted and cheerful attitude may not change our mood, but it certainly changes other people's.

Let's ask people how they feel, if they are worried, if we can do something for them. Let's listen to them.

Day after day, this habit will soon become a lifestyle. At first it will be difficult and terribly embarrassing, but in the long run these small gestures will make a difference.

Just start gradually. During the coffee break, for example; or at lunch, or any other daily opportunity.

Don't we all love being surrounded by positive people? Step by step, we can become a symbol of joy for others, a moment of relief, a space where they can feel safe and well. As a result, we will develop a better mood, and a much more positive approach to life. With just a little good will, and a lot of perseverance.

In order to achieve our goals, we must be the first to believe in them. Why should anyone believe in us, if we are the first to disbelieve in ourselves? Nobody will be willing to reward us for something we think we don't deserve in the first place.

TAKING RESPONSIBILITY

FOR OUR ACTIONS

*The more experience I gather, the more I realize that man himself
is the cause of his happiness as well as his misery.*
Mahatma Gandhi

While the attitudes we have just examined may be difficult to eliminate altogether, it is certainly within our reach to keep them in check. Our task, therefore, is to pay due attention to them.

Let's now take a look at the qualities that most virtuous attitudes have in common.

Have you ever noticed that successful people always take responsibility for their actions?

As we have seen before, once a challenge is identified, the human brain is programmed to find a solution. And the more we realize that we are the makers of our own destiny, the more this becomes true. As we begin to gain this awareness, our brain will spontaneously begin to identify the next steps to take.

I would like to focus on this innate ability, because it is of paramount importance. When the brain enters the search mode for the next step to take – when it tries to turn a problem into a challenge, and hope into action – we can sleep easy: the solution is around the corner. We needn't do anything else, because once the solution is found and understood, its fulfillment will be a natural step.

Basically, hope transforms difficulties into challenges, the brain strives to find the solution, and the solution is nothing more than a practical step towards improvement. As soon as the solution is identified, we move on to its implementation.

This will be right the time to take responsibility for your actions, since they will have repercussions as a consequence of the solution being implemented!

It may seem intricate, but once we understand this mechanism, we shall wonder how we didn't get it sooner. My advice is to read this chapter several times, and to try and visualize the different steps, until they become second nature.

THE MORNING ROUTINE

It's neither a magic potion, nor a weird definition. Having a precise morning routine, for even just a few minutes each day, makes all the difference! Setting aside a personal space to devote to any activities that make us happy, is the keystone of our day.

Our last thoughts before going to bed affect the way we sleep and, inevitably, also how we wake up, and the rest of our day.

Unfortunately, nowadays it's not at all uncommon to go directly from bed to cellphone mode, frantically reading the latest posts from Instagram, Facebook and what not.

Failing to stop and think about these bad habits, means we shall continue to live at the mercy of our thoughts, and of a routine that drags us day after day. On the contrary, a healthy and purpose-made routine can literally change our life.

So, let's take control of our thoughts and set up a mindful morning routine, full of activities that calm and enrich us. Let's start our day in peace, and feeling grateful for a new chapter in our life. Small thoughts and simple words of gratitude are incredibly powerful.

When we get up, let's smile and enjoy the scent of fresh coffee brewing, and cheering our heart even before we taste it. Let's give ourselves a treat, a favorite cookie for instance. We are alive, and we have a world of possibilities ahead of us; we are not castaways doomed to spend yet another nondescript day. The secret lies in these small actions. When performed with mindfulness and gratitude, they can change the course of our days in a surprising way!

CALLING PEOPLE BY THEIR NAME

We shouldn't fall into the trap of believing it's just a platitude.

Each one of us, deep down, considers him- or herself to be the most important person in the world, and more or less unconsciously we all think that everything revolves around us.

Let's implement this simple strategy: the next time we address someone, let's start by mentioning their name, and then continue with what we meant to say.

This trick won't just make them more alert to what we are going to say, but also much better inclined towards us. We made them feel important.

I remember certain work meetings, when I ended up getting bored, and drifted into my own thoughts. I was pretending to be focused, when in reality I couldn't have been further away. Suddenly someone mentioned my name, and all my senses were alert again, as if awakened by a whiplash, excited for being called upon directly.

SMILE, SMILE, SMILE

The most important decision you make
is to be in a good mood.
Voltaire

I will never stop urging people to smile!

People who take themselves too seriously, should really do some soul-searching.

We can learn to smile, to have facial expressions that resemble smiling rather than sulking.

Indeed, good mood also depends on some purely physiological aspects. In the central nervous system, for example, there is a neurotransmitter called serotonin, which regulates mood. Dopamine is another neurotransmitter associated with happiness. There are also endorphins, also known as "feel-good hormones" and 2-phenylethylamine, a hormone released in situations of emotional euphoria and excitement.

There are people who – simply by their presence – radiate an aura of good spirits all around them. Quite often, they are people with a great sense of humor and great respect for others. We can very well be ironic, and at the same time be very serious with our commitments. This is synonymous with balance, self-awareness, and great self-confidence.

EMBRACING DIVERSITY

Let us enrich ourselves with our mutual differences.
Paul Valéry

It takes all kinds to make a world, they say. Diversity is a wealth. Each one of us can learn something from others, in an uninterrupted, organic exchange of ideas, cultures, and habits.

Often, however, I come across people who just can't come to terms with diversity. Mind you, diversity is not necessarily of a cultural, religious or origin-related nature; it can also be just a different way of seeing things. It may be different ideas, or different interpretations. For example, it may be a manager who doesn't accept the unusual and original point of view of a young employee, and even refuses to listen to his ideas.

Albeit in different percentages, each of us can be a victim of this despotic attitude.

My first piece of practical advice is that you should admit the existence of this bias, then force yourself to listen to others, and finally to understand their perspective – or at least try. I advise you to do it gradually, so that your attention is not pretended or – even worse! – dictated by flattery. Gradually, it will become more and more authentic.

We should not be afraid to ask questions, especially if they are aimed at truly understanding the other's point of view. Then, let's try to rephrase what we heard, in our own words. The result will most likely be a constructive and truly bilateral discussion.

Finally, it is very important that we do not to fall into the trap of prejudice. Nobody holds the definitive truth, and nobody is always right – starting with us! Points of view may differ considerably, yet everyone has their reasons.

And luckily so.

Accepting diversity makes us better people, and enables us to establish a healthy, constructive and reciprocal exchange – be it cognitive, cultural, or of any other nature.

CHANGE IS THE ONLY POSSIBLE WAY

Hope is the thing with feathers -
That perches in the soul -
And sings the tune without the words -
And never stops - at all.
Emily Dickinson

We can change ourselves. However, it is not an overnight process. It requires commitment and practice, just like an athlete training for a race. Results come over time, and with consistent exercising.

Let's also remember that, contrary to common belief, any end results are not achieved only by virtue of our motivation, strong as it may be; rather, it's the first results that trigger a virtuous mechanism and push us to stay on course. This is what happens with diets, for example; but also in sports, music practice, or virtually any field in fact.

There is also another beneficial side-effect of trying to change ourselves: the results are only a fraction of the entire prize pool. During our journey we probably won't notice it, but even just trying to change, and working on ourselves, is an improvement in itself. It signifies that we have understood the meaning of hope, and the process that we have been discussing in this book: identify the problem; turn it into a challenge; take the necessary actions.

In other words, even when we believe that we have not achieved the expected results, as a matter of fact we have already achieved them. Bizarre, isn't it? These dynamics qualify as the path to success. Nothing is achieved without effort, by sitting comfortably on our sofa. Trials and failures are necessary, because they are the stones that pave our way to the finish line.

Let's face it, the words of successful people all have one message in common: Success is the son of Hope and Change, and only hard labor can give it birth.

The first step is changing ourselves; this will trigger changes in the wider world through an endless cycle of challenges and changes driven by the hope of making progress, day after day.

Ultimately, self-awareness and a yearning for personal development are essential to set out on a life-long learning path that will enable us not only to overcome the limits of our present, but to transform them into new skills in our toolkit for the future.

In fact, because of its fundamental importance, self-awareness is going to be the focus of my next e-book.

Contacts:
Kawtar.louahbi@icloud.com